Static

I0141035

Jimmy McAleavey

methuen | drama
LONDON • NEW YORK • OXFORD • NEW DELHI • SYDNEY

METHUEN DRAMA

Bloomsbury Publishing Plc, 50 Bedford Square, London, WC1B 3DP, UK
Bloomsbury Publishing Inc, 1385 Broadway, New York, NY 10018, USA
Bloomsbury Publishing Ireland, 29 Earlsfort Terrace, Dublin 2,
D02 AY28, Ireland

BLOOMSBURY, METHUEN DRAMA and the Methuen
Drama logo are trademarks of Bloomsbury Publishing Plc.

First published in Great Britain 2025

Image: Maaike Poels

Credit: AAD

A catalogue record for this book is available from the British Library.

Library of Congress Control Number: 2025939110

ISBN: PB: 978-1-3505-7947-7
ePDF: 978-1-3505-7949-1
eBook: 978-1-3505-7948-4

Series: Modern Plays

Typeset by Mark Heslington Ltd, Scarborough, North Yorkshire

For product safety related questions contact
productsafety@bloomsbury.com.

To find out more about our authors and books visit
www.bloomsbury.com and sign up for our newsletters.

World premiere

An Abbey Theatre production

Static

By Jimmy McAleavey

First performed on 20 June 2025 at the Abbey Theatre, Dublin

Directed by John King

Please note that the text of the play which appears in this volume may be changed during the rehearsal process and appear in a slightly altered form in performance.

CREATIVES

Moonman	**Dan Gordon**
Spaceman	**Seán Mahon**
Playwright	**Jimmy McAleavey**
Director	**John King**
Set and Costume Designer	**Alyson Cummins**
Lighting Designer	**Suzie Cummins**
Composer and Sound Designer	**Rob Moloney**
Hair and Make Up	**Val Sherlock**
Director of Voice and Actor Development	**Andrea Ainsworth**
Movement Director	**Gabrielle Moleta**
Casting Director	**Barry Coyle**
Production Researcher	**Dr Tanya Dean**

COMPANY

Producer	**Aoife McCollum**
Production Manager	**Andy Keogh**
Company Manager	**Danny Erskine**
Company Stage Manager	**Barbara Hughes**
Deputy Stage Manager	**Leanne Vaughey**
Costume Supervisor	**Yvonne Kelly**
Lighting Programmer	**Simon Burke**
Production Sound Technician	**Morgan Dunne**
Prop Master	**Adam O'Connell**
Set Construction	**Re-Staging**
Scenic Finishing	**Sandra Butler**
Marketing	**Muireann Kane** & **John Tierney**
Publicity	**Mia O'Reilly**
Digital Engagement	**Eva O'Beirne**
Artistic Director/Co-Director	**Caitríona McLaughlin**
Executive Director/Co-Director	**Mark O'Brien**

THE ABBEY THEATRE

As Ireland's national theatre, the Abbey Theatre's ambition is to enrich the cultural lives of everyone with a curiosity for and interest in Irish theatre, stories, artists and culture. Courage and imagination are at the heart of our storytelling, while inclusivity, diversity and equality are at the core of our thinking. Led by Co-Directors Caitríona McLaughlin (Artistic Director) and Mark O'Brien (Executive Director), the Abbey Theatre celebrates both the rich canon of Irish dramatic writing and the potential of future generations of Irish theatre artists.

Ireland has a rich history of theatre and playwriting and extraordinary actors, designers and directors. Artists are at the heart of our organization, with Marina Carr and Conor McPherson as Senior Associate Playwrights and Caroline Byrne as Associate Director.

Our stories teach us what it is to belong, what it is to be excluded and to exclude. Artistically our programme is built on twin impulses, and around two questions: 'who we were, and who are we now?'. We interrogate our classical canon with an urgency about what makes it speak to this moment. On our stages we find and champion new voices and new ways of seeing, our purpose – to identify combinations of characters we are yet to meet, having conversations we are yet to hear.

abbeytheatre.ie

the arts council schomhairle ealaion funding theatre

ABBEY THEATRE SUPPORTERS

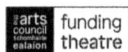

arts council / funding theatre

OLLSCOIL na GAILLIMHE
UNIVERSITY OF GALWAY

An Roinn Turasóireachta, Cultúir,
Ealaíon, Gaeltachta, Spóirt agus Meán
Department of Tourism, Culture,
Arts, Gaeltacht, Sport and Media

PROGRAMME PARTNER

RTÉ SUPPORTING arts

CORPORATE GUARDIANS

Bloomberg   ESB

Irish Life   NORTHERN TRUST

RETAIL PARTNER

ARNOTTS

GOLD AMBASSADORS

Ipsos B&A   ecclesiastical

Goodbody   McCANN FITZGERALD

FLYNN HODKINSON

HOSPITALITY PARTNER

THE WESTBURY
THE DOYLE COLLECTION · DUBLIN

IT PARTNER

Qualcom

SILVER AMBASSADOR

interpath   ODGERS BERNDTSON

wines direct

RESTAURANT PARTNERS

HAWKSMOOR   NANNETTI'S
CUCINA ITALIANA

GUARDIANS

The Cielinski Family
Deirdre and Irial Finan
Carmel and Martin Naughton
Sheelagh O'Neill
Donal Moore R.I.P.

VISIONARIES

Tony Ahearne
Pat and Kate Butler
Janice Flynn
Susan and Denis Tinsley

INNOVATORS

Gerard and Liv McNaughton
Louise Richardson R.I.P.

CHAMPION

Tommy Gibbons
Eugene Magee
Andrew and Delyth Parkes

CREATORS

Cathy Allen
Frances Britton
Margaret Roohan

EXPLORERS

Valerie Cole
Thelma Doran
Peter Howlett
Mary and Kevin Hoy
John Gabriel Irwin
Anne Lardener
Janet O'Brien
Tina Robinson
Kathleen Walsh

We want to thank the listed supporters for their ongoing generosity and belief in Ireland's National Theatre. We would also like to thank our generous supporters who have asked to remain anonymous.

Static

For Jarlath Benson

Characters

Moonman, *a middle-aged man from Donegal.*
Spaceman, *a middle-aged man from America.*

Content Warning: *Strong Language*

Scene One

Sound of static. **Spaceman** *is adjusting his seat with a spanner, trying to get it into a more comfortable position. He gives up. Pilot comfort is not an option.*

His breathing escalates and he tries to control it with a technical mantra.

Spaceman CO_2 levels . . . check.

Tank pressure . . . check.

Barometrics . . . check.

Trim and alignment . . . check.

Initiate hatch de-pressure . . . Three, ok. Two, ok. One, ok
. . . and hatch re-pressure, one and two and . . .

Little Earth appears at the window.

. . . Earth . . . check.

Little blue ball. Check.

He's trying to talk himself into it . . .

Little Christmas bauble.

Fragile robin's egg.

. . . with increasing success . . .

Precious Fabergé egg. Precious.

. . . then failure. He grabs an old-fashioned two-way short-wave radio and puts the headphones on. Static. It calms him. He breathes into it. He mimics the static, saying 'shush', shushing himself, the world, the universe.

Shusshhhhhhhhhh . . .

Scene Two

Black. Black. Black. Fade up the sound of static.

Fade up **Moonman**, *lit by the green screen of his vintage wave oscillator, seated in a wheelchair, headset attached to an old-fashioned ham radio. Winter dusk outside.*

Moonman   Yvan? Yvan? Your old friend from Donegal here, over?

Static in reply.

Over?

Switching to short wave, Yvan. Back your end of the dial in a mo.

He tunes to a separate band or frequency.

Judeska! What's the craic? Did you get the new truck?

Judeska? Still eating up the old autostrada?

Judeska, over?

He tunes again.

Yvan? I'm back, over?

Static.

Hang on, I'll get back to you, right? Promise, over.

He retunes.

Manuel! Manuel, over? Manuel, you Spanish rascal! What about your woman with the hump? Did she ever get up again? Over?

Over?

You're not . . . you lot haven't fallen out with me? . . . you know . . . the other day . . . I was only joking . . .

Static.

Get back to you, amigo. Promised I'd check in with Yvan. (*Whispers.*) I think that old trouble he has is back . . .

Re-tunes.

Yvan? Yvan? Over?

Static. It makes him panicky.

For company, he tunes in to a numbers station – The Lincolnshire Poacher with its bizarre folk tune followed by a voice reading seemingly random numbers. He switches to the 'Russian Man' station reading out numbers in Russian. He tunes into another: the Cuban numbers station with its numbers being read out followed by its strange gong. He tries to relax into it, miming the numbers.

Scene Three

Black. Black. Fade up all the stars in the sky.

From above: Beep . . . Beep . . . Beep.

We see **Spaceman**, *reciting his calming mantra.*

Spaceman CO_2 levels? Check.

Tank pressure? Check.

Barometrics? . . .

Mission Control on **Earth** *comes through the comms* (*separate to his old short-wave ham radio*).

Earth   BB174, ID code alpha . . . tango . . . tango . . . six. Are you receiving?

Silence.

Spaceman   . . . check.

Earth   Good to talk to you, Commander.

Let's get this thing started.

CO_2 levels?

Spaceman   Check.

Earth   Tank pressure?

Spaceman   Check.

Earth   Barometrics?

Spaceman   Check.

Earth   OK. That's a go.

Time to bring you home! Word is there's a gold watch for you here, and Franziska says you can smoke that touchdown cigar in the control room!

Stand by for landing initiation code.

Spaceman   Reserve tank pressure . . .

Earth   Standing by for landing initiation code? Over?

Spaceman   . . . check.

Earth   Sending landing initiation code.

Silence.

Sending landing initiation code. Over?

Silence.

Spaceman   Initiate hatch de-pressure . . .

Earth   Are you receiving landing initiation code? Over?

Spaceman   Three, ok. Two, ok. One, ok . . .

Earth   Are you receiving?

Spaceman   . . . and re-pressure. One, ok. Two, ok . . .

Earth   Are you –

Spaceman *impulsively grabs the spanner and bashes the comms panel with three fierce blows.*

Spaceman   Comms disconnected? Check.

Silence? Check.

Peace? Check?

Silence. Check. Silence. Check. Silence . . .

Space.

Time. To . . . [think]

We hear him breathe across space, in, out. Space. Space. Space . . .

A sensor starts to beep. He silences it. Another starts.

Shut up! Shut up!

Spaceman *hauls his old ham radio out and puts its headphones on. He turns the dial until he hears static in a bid to drown out the noise.*

Scene Four

The calming effect of the numbers stations subsides and **Moonman**'s *anxiety returns. He retunes.*

Moonman   Yvan? Yvan, over?

Morse code comes over the radio. It keeps repeating the same phrase.

Hang on, Yvan. Hang on a minute.

He writes down the corresponding letters.

K . . . O . . . V . . .

Hang on, Yvan – bit rusty. Give us a chance . . .

The Morse code phrase keeps repeating.

K. O. V . . . F . . . . . . U . . .

Kovfu? Ah now, Yvan, you know I don't speak Russian.

The code repeats.

Ah, got you . . . F. U. K. O. V.

Fewkov. Now I know I should learn Russian, I mean everyone should, but . . . fewkoff . . . ah . . . that's charming Yvan . . . that's really . . . wee joke, eh? Wee Russian joke, eh?

The code stops, then starts again with deliberate emphasis.

You're . . .! You're a . . .!

You're not yourself, Yvan. No, you're not yourself. I'll check in with you tomorrow, see how you're doing.

Moonman *retunes.*

Manuel, over? Me old buddy, Manuel, over?

Static. **Moonman** *sits in static. He's so lonely he might cry.*

Judeska . . .

Judeska, over?

Judeska . . . please . . .

Oh why don't you all . . . [fuck off] you're all so smart with your . . . (*sneers*) *lives*!

He switches on a domestic FM radio to shut out his thoughts. Music.

Scene Five

Earth *comes into* **Spaceman**'s *view.*

Spaceman   Little blue miracle.

Jewel of the Milky Way.

Little blue-eye.

Don't give me the come on, baby; I know what you are.

He is momentarily seduced again . . .

Tiny . . . put my thumb on you.

Then his bitterness returns . . .

Rub you . . . the fuck out.

He looks away from Earth, out to space, perhaps out a second window. He feels fear, incipient terror even, but talks himself out of it.

No – wonder.

Wonder. Check.

He can't quite get the rhythm of his breathing.

No.

Awe.

Check.

Awe.

We see **Moonman** *sitting holding his ham radio mic, in front of his FM radio. The dong of the Angelus bell comes through* **Spaceman***'s ham radio.*

Spaceman   What the fuck!?

He looks all around him in panic, including out the window. **Moonman** *jumps as he hears* **Spaceman***'s voice.*

Moonman *says tentatively into his mic:*

Moonman   Hello?

Spaceman *hears this strange voice – it could be anything; it could be the voice of God.*

Moonman   Hello?

Spaceman *whips his headphones off, scared.*

Moonman   Hello?

Spaceman *puts the headset back on, tentative but curious.*

Moonman   Over?

Spaceman   . . . Over?

Moonman   Receiving, over.

Spaceman   You're receiving, over?

Moonman   Wall-to-wall and treetop-tall!

Spaceman   International Space Station?

Moonman   Pardon me?

Spaceman   Starliner? Wentian?

Moonman   What?

Spaceman   . . . Earth?

Moonman   What?

Spaceman   Are you on Earth?

Moonman *is puzzled.*

Moonman   In a manner of speaking. Donegal. Ireland, top left pocket.

Spaceman   Why can't you, why can't you all, why can't you just, just for a second, why can't you all just shut up?!

Moonman   . . . Right.

I'll be quiet so.

A thought occurs to **Spaceman**.

Spaceman   Are you Digistar telecoms?

He types into his computer, looks at screens – he's trying to locate **Moonman**.

Moonman   . . . That would be a negatory . . . Digistar Telecoms? That a satellite company?

More typing.

Spaceman (*to self*)   Satellite monitoring.

He narrows it down to Europe.

Least it's not the Russians.

Moonman   Was on the Sky package once . . .

Static creeps in. **Moonman** *adjusts his tuner.*

Moonman   Having antenna problems there?

Spaceman   What do you know about my comms? Sky Package? That a European affiliate of Digistar?

Moonman   Putting the satellites up? That the story?

Spaceman   There is no story. There is nothing wrong with my comms. Are you media?

Moonman   Me?

Spaceman (*to self*)   Fucking listening station . . . Chinese . . . fucking everywhere . . .

He keeps narrowing down his signal, needs to keep him on the line.

Moonman   Just . . .

If you want a bit of peace and quiet . . .

I'll head on here . . .

He won't. He sits back.

Spaceman   Hang on . . .

Spaceman *is closing in on him.*

Moonman   But . . .

If you want a bit of peace and quiet . . . why do you have your radio on?

Spaceman   Static, ok?! I like to listen to . . . nothing, OK?

(*To self.*) Ireland?

Moonman   I suppose . . . sometimes I would like to open the windows . . . listen to . . . But static, it's not nothing.

Spaceman   You can't get nothing, ok? Even here, especially here, all you can hear are your own . . . [thoughts].

Moonman   And where did you say that was?

Spaceman   Static is the closest thing to nothing in the universe, ok? Background cosmic radiation, echo of the Big Bang, ok? Closest we can get to *nothing* before there was all *this* . . . noise!

Moonman   Right. Get you.

Spaceman   So what are you doing on this frequency?! No one uses this frequency!

Moonman   Oh, police, is it? American police? 'Please be careful out there.'

Spaceman   I am not the police.

He locates **Moonman**'s *signal in County Donegal.*

Who the hell are you?!

Moonman   Oh, that was rude of me. My handle is Moonman, I have a 20 in a stack-o'-bricks in Ireland, between rigs at the minute, but doing a bit of sandbagging on the triple nickel.

Well, my 10-20 is –

Spaceman   You're just . . . some guy?

Moonman   Me? I'm just a fella, likes to talk to truckers, whatever they're hauling there: satellite dishes –

Spaceman   Dishes?

Moonman   Frozen goods . . . *confidential cargo* . . .

Spaceman   Uh-huh?

He's trying to get a precise fix.

Moonman   I know about peace and quiet all right . . . I live in the countryside way in the middle of nowhere where nobody lives, in a county called Donegal where nobody really lives, in a country called Ireland where nobody in their right mind lives.

Spaceman *gets a precise fix, relaxes.*

Moonman   See, a man could walk out his door here and just keep walking. First across the bog. Just you and the snipe. Do you know what they call a bunch of snipe? A wisp. That's a good one for a quiz.

Spaceman (*to himself*)   Well, well . . .

Moonman   Then on up the mountain and the wind whistling and the larks rising, all the way up to the coolin.

Spaceman (*to himself*)   Isn't that just typical?

Moonman   Just sit by the water and just be content, and the wind and the larks and let it all seep slowly into you. You'd love it.

Spaceman (*to himself*)   Typical my little blue-eyed whore.

Moonman   A man could lose himself in this country. A man could give himself the slip.

Spaceman   Ha! You see, with a little tweak, this old bucket can track your signal and it says –

Moonman   You *are* a trucker! Driving some fancy new rig there, buddy?

Spaceman   Hmmm. Twin OMS boosters, cross-linkable. Monomethyl hydrazine propulsion.

Moonman   Sounds hard on the old motion lotion! Careful! There's a Kojak with a Kodak every mile on the way to Ballybofey!

Spaceman   No, you see, this thing can pinpoint your signal. I can see your house from here. Granted, you've about two acres of field around you, but you don't live in the countryside; you live on the edge of a small city. 'Letterkenny', it says here.

Moonman   Ah, you see –

Spaceman   No, my question is this: why does someone reach across space to talk, then starts the conversation with a lie? The point is: what *is it* about people?

He tunes **Moonman** *out abruptly. We're with* **Moonman** *on his own now.*

Moonman   No, see it's *like* I live in the country. It's *like* . . . and, you know, in the winter, you know the days they'd be dim here. And you'd wake up maybe . . . and you wouldn't know whether it was dawn or dusk or the middle of the day . . .

Over?

Static from **Spaceman**.

Moonman   And you wouldn't have talked to anyone maybe for . . . like the way they *would do* in the country. Over?

And then the streetlights, see, would go off at one in the morning, and maybe you'd be sitting up in bed, looking through the skylight at the stars. There's your stars for you.

And you're supposed to . . . you, know, the 'wonder of the' . . .

No?

Over?

Static. He gives up on **Spaceman**.

Moonman   . . . looking at the stars and you would be like maybe a bachelor farmer and all belonging to you gone, the *silence*, and you're supposed to look up at the stars and go – *wow, isn't it all so –*

But what if he's looking up into space – the bachelor farmer – and it being . . . bigger than huger than vast, colder than absolute zero that's vaster than cold . . . and maybe he's not looking at the stars, twinkle, twinkle, *bloody twinkle*, but the space between them. And then he's in it, and it's in his chest: absolute zero colder than infinite nothing than darker than black. In his *eyeballs*. And it crushing his lungs, absolute infinite zero of black and absolute nothing of silent would burst your eardrums.

You know that way?

There's your bloody stars for you.

Spaceman *is faint, but we reveal that he has been listening.*

Spaceman   Don't talk to me about loneliness! Loneliness is my job.

Moonman   Jesus!

Spaceman   Don't tell *me* about space!

Moonman *scrambles to get his headset off, crippled by embarrassment.*

Absolute colder than darker than fucker than – crush your ribcage like a Coke can, suffocate you, suck your eyeballs out of your fucking head!

He switches the set off. **Moonman** *is not a threat, but he has terrified him. Desperately, he tries to reclaim his previous fragile equanimity.*

Spaceman   Awe.

Alarms spring to life and he tries to silence them in sequence.

Awe!

He pulls the cover off the comms panel.

A smiling woman's voice starts:

Computer   Oxygen!

Spaceman   Awe!

Computer   Oxygen!

Spaceman   Awe!

Computer   Oxygen!

Spaceman   Awe!

Computer   Oxygen AOK!

The panel goes on fire. **Spaceman** *uses a fire extinguisher on it.*

Spaceman   Aw, what the fuck have you done?!

Hopelessly, he tries the comms.

Starburst alpha-alpha-six, ID code seven, seven, beta. Are you receiving?

BB174, are you receiving?

Control, are you receiving?

Can you hear me?

Silence.

He turns to the comms panel, probes the mess inside, returns to the ham radio.

This is an SOS. Over?

Static.

This is a Mayday.

Over!

He scrolls through frequencies.

Irishman, over?

Irishman, over?

Are you receiving, over?

Are you receiving?

Moonman *emerges from the static.*

Moonman   10-4 there, mystery man! I wanted to talk to you.

Spaceman   Great. I need you to do something for me.

Moonman   See it's *like* I live in the country.

Spaceman   Never mind about that; we all got issues.

Moonman   Pardon me?

Spaceman   I've got issues. I've got an issue right now, so I need you to make a phone call for me. This could work out very nicely for you.

Moonman   No, see, it's *like* I live in the country –

Spaceman   Financially? Maybe. But I really need you to do it now.

Moonman   Great. Only too pleased – but see it's like I live in the country because I wouldn't get out much.

See, my 10-20 is –

Spaceman   Can we pause the CB-talk for a second? I mean like park it up. In the truck stop.

Moonman   Copy that. Park the bear crap in the nap trap.

Spaceman   Stop it!

Moonman   . . . 10-4.

Spaceman *bites his tongue.*

Spaceman   Now you could come out of this very well. Some kind of reward. You know what an NDA is? They might ask you to sign something – but some kind of discreet reward would be appropriate. And what I am asking of you is very simple.

Moonman   Wow . . . No . . .

Spaceman   No?

Moonman   No, I wouldn't get out much now.

Spaceman *succumbs to irritation.*

Spaceman   What, are you like the Elephant Man or something?

Moonman   Ah now, no. It's on account of my rig.

Spaceman   Your rig?

Moonman   The old fireside Ferrari, the old Lourdes skateboard.

Spaceman   The what?

Moonman   Two-bun truck-hauling ass!

Spaceman   You're not in a – [wheelchair]

Moonman   I use a wheelchair.

Spaceman   Shit.

Moonman   See, so it's a bit like living out in the country.

Spaceman   That doesn't matter. It's just a phone call.

Static starts to creep in.

Moonman   Hang on, need to re-tune here . . . it's like you're moving . . . have to keep retuning – God but you're motoring!

Spaceman   It's line-of-sight. It's when I'm passing over, every twelve hours, give or take, depending on atmospheric conditions down there. We should have a few more minutes . . .

Moonman   Passing over?

He re-tunes again.

What on earth are you driving there – sorry, what's your handle?

Spaceman   Now I accept you might find this difficult to believe but I'm not on a CB. I'm looking out here at the stars here. I'm not driving a truck, *good buddy*.

Moonman   Oh, sorry, get mixed up – I have Citizens' Band, full ham-radio set-up, even do the old Morse code . . . what are you broadcasting on there?

Spaceman   This is relevant. It's some old short-wave set another guy left here, *along with two half-empty jars of peanut butter*, even though it was ticked off the decant list . . . used it to talk to schoolkids, I think.

Moonman   Oh . . . prison, is it? Looking out at the stars? No, you're moving, of course . . . like a bloody freight train.

Spaceman   That's because I am aboard the Starburst VI spacecraft in mid-Earth orbit 21,545 miles from Earth travelling at approximately three miles per second.

My name is Commander Slane, ex-United States Air Force, ex-NASA, now with Digistar Technologies. And all I need you to do is make a phone call.

Moonman   Oh, ho-ho!

Ho-ho!

Friend of Yvan's, are you?

Spaceman   I don't know what you mean, unless it's like 'friend of Dorothy' or something.

Moonman   Who's Dorothy?

Spaceman   The thing is we don't have very much time here . . . I'm passing overhead and we only have a small window for communication.

Moonman   Did Judeska put you up to this? Ho-ho! She's a funny girl, that one!

Spaceman   And I'm pretty sure I'm running out of O_2 here, no matter what anybody says, and I *know* I'm going to run out of fuel and –

Moonman   Uh-huh. Who was the first American in space?

Spaceman   What? Alan Shepard.

Moonman   Who stayed in the command and support module in the first Apollo landing?

Spaceman   Mike Collins. Command module, not a CSM.

Moonman   Who was the last person to set foot on the Moon?

Spaceman   The *latest* person to stand on the Moon was Jack Schmitt.

Moonman   Now I wouldn't say to a man I didn't believe him . . . but just . . . me with every book written about space flight. With all the Apollo mission badges my Aunt Peggy sent over from Florida all sewn on my parka. So a man might think it's a coincidence that he's sitting in the house, little me in my rig, and next I'm talking to a . . . colossus of the bloody cosmos. How *would* a man know a man wasn't making this all up?

Spaceman   Because I can see your house from here. I got a lock on your signal. I can call up satellite pictures, zoom into your back yard. Can't do that in a truck.

And I really need you to make a phone call for me so I can initiate landing sequence and get to the nearest bar before I get sucked into . . . infinite darkness . . . of zero of black.

Moonman   You can see my house?

Spaceman   You have a window in the roof, a roof light.

Moonman *switches the light off.*

Spaceman   Off.

Moonman *switches it back on.*

Spaceman   On.

Moonman *starts to mess around with intervals of on and off.*

Is that . . . Morse code? Hang on . . .

Moonman *repeats the sequence. Then again.*

Spaceman   Fewkov?

Moonman *is stunned, tempted to believe.*

Spaceman   What's that supposed to mean?

Moonman   Are you up the mountain? With a telescope?

Spaceman   No, I am not up a mountain, or a big ladder, or a particularly tall tree. I am in mid-Earth orbit . . . until I run out of fuel, get rear-ended by any of thirty-one GPS satellites in similar orbits and spin out into space!

Moonman   Roger. Roger that.

Spaceman   And all I am asking you to do is make a telephone call.

Moonman   Ah, you see . . .

. . . you've got me there. Even if you were an astronaut stranded in space, I couldn't phone Cape Canaveral or wherever. No mobile. Sorry, *cell phone*.

Spaceman   Landline then.

Moonman   Ah there was a whole mix-up with the bill. See what happened was this: they offered me this friends and family plan, but *I* said –

Spaceman   You can tell me all about it after you've got hold of someone in authority. Honestly, I look forward to that, but if you could just walk out your door – I mean wheel yourself outside and go to the nearest police station . . .

Moonman   Righty-ho. Roger that.

Just . . . why can't you call them yourself? Not on this old yoke, of course, nobody uses this anymore.

Spaceman   Can you just – [listen for a moment]

Moonman   And of course if they don't know you have a short-wave radio, then they're not going to be trying to get the hold of you on it.

It starts to dawn on **Moonman** *that he has him all to himself.*

But why don't you just speak to them on your whatchamacallit?

Spaceman   There's been a comms malfunction.

Moonman   Comms, that's it.

You have a back-up surely.

Spaceman   That's gone down too.

Moonman   That's terrible luck.

Like, in a *spacecraft*.

Spaceman   Could you please?

Moonman   I mean if you had, say, a landline and a mobile phone, and they both stopped working . . . that would be really bad luck.

But like *in a spacecraft*.

Some people would find that hard to believe . . .

They'd say that would all have to be . . . 'shielded' would be the word.

Spaceman   Whipple shields, alloy farings, multi-layer anti-radiation insulation blankets . . . but sometimes the . . . non-nominal . . . happens.

Moonman   The what?

Spaceman   The unanticipated.

Moonman   What, like an accident? Oh no! What happened?

Spaceman   It's hard to explain. I really need you to –

Static grows.

Moonman   Oh, is it *technical*?

Spaceman   Yes, it's technical!

Moonman   Would I not *understand it*?

Spaceman   I hit the comms panel with a wrench! Technically, a *space wrench*. OK?

Moonman   What did you do that for?

Spaceman   Could you please, *please*, do what I asked?

Moonman   What do you want me to tell them again?

Static.

Spaceman   Tell them . . . tell them . . .

Moonman   Nope. Losing you.

Static overwhelms **Spaceman**.

Moonman   Are you there? Are you receiving?

Static.

An astronaut?

An astronaut!

A real-life bloody astronaut!

He whoops.

A double-barrelled, twenty-four-carat, real-life bloody astronaut!

He whoops. He stands up out of his wheelchair and whoops.

Scene Six

Spaceman *is typing stuff into a computer and studying what comes up.*

Spaceman   Re-entry window?

Closing. Check.

Horizon for absolute loss of control . . .

Based on current fuel . . .

4.87 . . . 3 . . . 8 . . . 6 6 repeating . . . orbits . . .

He sets up an orbit countdown on a laptop. Sometimes we might see its fractions ticking down.

His breathing starts to get out of control.

O$_2$?

AOK. For now.

We hear **Moonman** *fight through static through the ham radio. He's bolt upright at his SW radio, wearing his space parka.*

Moonman   Calling Spaceman. Are you receiving?

Are you receiving, over?

Spaceman   Receiving, over. Did you do what I / asked?

Moonman   About the other night /

Spaceman   / contact / someone?

Moonman   / Laid it on a bit thick about space.

Spaceman   Did you?

Moonman   I did, yeah.

Like a poem, you know. A wee poem. We would do that here.

Spaceman   Did you go to the police station?

Moonman   Ah no, too far. Pishing down out there. State of the lane . . .

Spaceman   You spoke to someone in authority?

Moonman   I did, yeah.

And the price of tarmac these days. Time was the Travellers would – [call]

Spaceman   You spoke to someone?

Moonman   I did, yeah.

Spaceman   Who?

Moonman   I did, yeah.

Spaceman   In authority?

Moonman   Postman, yeah.

Spaceman   Christ, I know he wears a uniform and all, but –

Moonman   He's going to send the Guards out – police, yeah.

Just waiting for them to call out.

Tell me, how long did you train for? To become an astronaut. Tell me. Couple of minutes. While we're waiting.

They're coming, all right. I spoke to him.

They'd be on his round.

I mean it's not every day you meet – [an astronaut] tell me, did you always want to be an astronaut?

Spaceman *decides he'd better keep this guy onside.*

Spaceman   You like that stuff, yeah?

Moonman   You betcha!

Spaceman   My feet were always itchy on Earth. When I was a kid I did a moonwalk in a swamp wearing my father's hunting boots. When I was let out of the house again I got some rope and a bucket and sent our cat into geostatic orbit round a tree.

Moonman   Did you get shouted at?

Spaceman   My dad was pissed, but my mom always thought I was destined for great things. Had me very late.

Moonman   Snap!

Spaceman   Well, there you go! Heaven-sent and all that.

Moonman   You've been trying to get home!

Spaceman   What? Yes, exactly, I'm trying to get home.

Moonman   No, I meant up the way – never mind.

Spaceman   Any sign there, buddy?

Moonman   No . . . not yet.

Go on, how'd you become an astronaut?

Spaceman   Air Force, NASA, five years later got my PhD in aeronautics. My body mass index is 21. I have never slept longer than six hours.

Moonman   See, you're special.

Spaceman   Yeah. Special.

He's not anymore. He tries to be chipper.

If Neil and Buzz hadn't gone to the Moon I'd probably have become a Shaolin monk.

You'll hear the cops when they call by, yeah?

Moonman   You know Neil Armstrong and Buzz Aldrin?

Spaceman   They both attended my lecture on future fuels.

Moonman   What was that like?

Spaceman   Successful. It's not so much the fuel, although that has a lot to do with it, but – in layman's terms – trying to re-employ the exhaust vector somehow.

Moonman   No – what are *they* like? Neil and Buzz.

Spaceman   They're . . . astronauts . . . talk about astronaut stuff. Keep their weight down.

Moonman   Oh.

Spaceman   You'll hear them ok?

Moonman   Couldn't be long now. Tell me, did you ever go on a spacewalk? That must be the scariest thing ever – floating in space.

Spaceman   You're tethered. And you've a job to do.

Moonman   But it would take some gumption.

Spaceman We're trained for EVAs and, as I say, you're focused on the task . . . but . . . just at the moment the hatch shuts behind you . . . you're not part of the crew anymore, part of the ship. Staring out at infinite space.

Moonman Space, you staring into infinite space.

Nobody knows where it starts or where it ends. Would frighten an ordinary man.

Spaceman Yeah. Strange though. Part of you wants to . . .

Pause. This is relevant to the here and now.

Moonman What?

Spaceman Float off into it.

Moonman *What?*

Spaceman Like *Voyager 1*, out there on its own! But then you gotta get your wrenches out without sending one off on the slow train to Jupiter. Zero gravity, nuts seem to loosen as soon as they're tightened. You want to maybe go check –

Moonman Ah, I think you're being a bit modest.

Spaceman Well, maybe astronauts don't make a big deal of things. Give us a choice between a spacewalk and a job in a bank . . .

Moonman Not like ordinary mortals, eh? Not like the likes of us, eh? Earth-bound. *Wheelchair*-bound.

Spaceman You can be special, but not forever.

Moonman Chalk and cheese. Shite and dynamite.

Spaceman What do you say you just go outside and check?

Moonman Sure they'll be here in a minute.

I have all the books on space flight, you know! You know, while we're – waiting. Tell us –

Spaceman   What did he say, the postman? He was going straight there, yeah?

Moonman   It was a brief conversation.

Spaceman   What did he say?

Moonman   I couldn't quite make him out.

Spaceman   What, are you deaf as well?

Moonman   Well, now, that doesn't make any sense. If I was deaf I couldn't listen to you, could I? God, imagine – [if I was deaf and all]

Spaceman   What do you mean you couldn't hear him?

Moonman   Through the letterbox.

Spaceman *is speechless for a moment.*

But I told him to send them out. Quite clearly. They're trained for that kind of thing here.

Spaceman   Astronautical emergencies?!

Moonman   To keep an eye. Send people out to the house if necessary.

Spaceman *bites his tongue. He realises he's going to have to play this smarter.*

Spaceman   Yeah, but you must have people come by, as well? Check up on you? Physical therapy, yeah?

Moonman   Oh I have people. Pair of women live up the town – sisters.

Spaceman   Oh yeah? When do they – [call]

Moonman   Pick me up a few bits and pieces. Drop me in my tablets. Antoinette's not well though; mightn't see them for a wee while.

Tell us about the first, the Mercury Seven, while we're waiting.

Spaceman *takes a moment to consider, then steps it up.*

Spaceman   You read about the Mercury Seven? You like that stuff?

Moonman   Rock 'n' roll!

Spaceman   Gus Grissom and the gang. Gold Italian suits.

Moonman   Matching gold Corvettes!

Spaceman   You like that, yeah? One big party for the passing of the old world before the bringing in of the new. Test-flying, fast girls, fast cars, smoke a big Habano on touchdown.

Moonman   That's the job, *that's* what I'm talking about.

Spaceman   And their mission? Answer the Big Questions.

What's out there? God? Infinity? Is *this it*?

No beard-stroking in some hippy cafe, just climb on a rocket and hang on. Jock philosophers every one. The greatest American you could be.

Moonman   Greatest men!

Spaceman   When I get home, I'm going to get me a gold suit. I'm going to get them to send you a gold suit.

Moonman   Ha!

Spaceman   Get one of those sisters to help you on with the pants.

Moonman   I don't need any help with my trousers, thank you. Michaela?!

Spaceman   Or off . . .

Moonman   Antoinette?! She's near eighty.

Spaceman   Yeah, you struck me as an independent kind of guy. Encounter challenge? Check. Overcome it? Check.

Moonman *knows he's being patronised.*

So what do you say you go out there and just flag someone down?

Moonman   Stop someone on the road? 'I wonder would you mind calling into the Guards for me as I have a buddy stranded in space?'

Spaceman   Resourceful guy like you –

Moonman (*more bitterly*)   They'd be going: 'You know your man lives in the big field on the Derry Road, never goes out, well he's gone completely loo-la now. The *poor creature*, I always said it was just a matter of time.'

Spaceman   Tell them you got broken into! Tell them your dog caught fire!

Moonman   Now, now. Tell me about *your* mission.

Spaceman   What do you know about my mission?

Moonman   Ah, now, no need to be tetchy. I understand why it's secret. Budget. The government are afraid people will complain.

Spaceman   I'm not supposed to be up here this long . . . I've got about four more go-arounds before we start playing astronaut pinball.

Moonman   But this journalist noticed big budget increases like in forestry management. Or researching new strains of wheat. Except it's all going to the space programme on the QT.

Spaceman   And, as for O_2 in here . . .

Moonman   Ah, I see, you don't want to talk about it. You're not supposed to talk about it.

Spaceman   I can feel it running out . . . O_2.

Moonman   What does your dial say?

Spaceman   My *dial?*! My dial is stuck on full, ok?! Things go wrong in spacecraft you know! They're not like cars. You can't test thousands of them to destruction!

Moonman   Ah it wouldn't get stuck, now. They'd have the full of WD40 in that.

Spaceman*'s breathing is laboured now.*

Spaceman   I can feel it! I'm running out of oxygen!

Moonman   Ah, you're having a panic attack.

Spaceman   A panic attack? I'm a fucking astronaut!

Moonman   Have you a paper bag?

Spaceman   In a *spacecraft*?

Moonman   You have peanut butter.

Of course, though, you're an *astronaut*.

He's enjoying the role reversal.

Astronauts don't get panic attacks, no.

Course they don't smash their spaceships up either . . .

Spaceman   I NEED YOU TO GET ME DOWN FROM HERE!

Moonman   Now!

Now.

Slow your breathing down.

There's nothing to be afraid of.

It's all in your head.

Spaceman   It's not in my head! It's out there! Space, remember?! Infinite zero of blacker than colder than fucker than dark! Remember?

Moonman   Oh. That.

Spaceman   All I need is for you to get me a code. A code is sent to initiate re-entry. Given the damage suffered, I cannot receive said code. All I need is for you to talk to someone in authority to talk to Digistar to get me someone with said code.

He glances at his countdown clock . . .

And in just short of twelve hours we will talk again and you will give me someone with said code!

Static starts to drown him out.

Moonman   Losing you there . . .

Static.

Scene Seven

Moonman *is poised for* **Spaceman** *to call, checking in repeatedly on the ham radio. Nothing. He flicks the speaker/remote mic switch on the ham radio (no headset required) and on his long-wave set listens to one of his numbers stations (The Lincolnshire Poacher or Cherry Ripe) to block out the silence.*

Spaceman *flicks his speaker switch. He listens, sussing* **Moonman** *out.* **Spaceman** *hears the numbers station, maybe jots down the numbers being read. He's at the very least sceptical of* **Moonman** *contacting the authorities.*

Moonman *tires of the numbers station, switches to FM.*

Presenter   One death notice this evening. McGovern, Antoinette.

Moonman   Ah, no . . .

Presenter   Peacefully at home after a short illness. Her blessed remains will be interred on Friday after 10 o'clock mass. And a lovely poem from her sister, Michaela. 'You were a rose with every perfect petal, whene'er I called you put on the kettle.'

Spaceman   One of the sisters?

Moonman *jumps.*

Moonman   Wasn't well lately. Just Michaela now.

Suppose I'd be all she has left now.

Spaceman *might raise an eyebrow at this.*

Spaceman   Take it they're not there then.

Moonman   Who?

Spaceman   The Boise Idaho Quilting Circle! Who?! Whoever's in charge down there.

Moonman   Nothing yet.

Spaceman   No.

Moonman   AOK. They're coming out.

Spaceman   Course.

Moonman   How's the O_2 situation?

Spaceman O_2? AOK. For now.

What was that you were listening to?

Moonman   That? Oh that. Numbers station.

Spaceman   A what?

Moonman   It's just this one reading out numbers. And then their wee tune. Then the numbers again.

Spaceman   That sounds very like cipher to me.

Moonman   Yeah, people say it has to do with spies and secret codes and all, but I don't know.

Spaceman   What have you got it on for?

Moonman   Oh, you know . . .

Spaceman   No, I don't know.

Moonman   It's always there, day or night.

Spaceman   But why listen to it?

Moonman   For, you know . . . the numbers.

Spaceman   The numbers?

Moonman   The . . . like you and your static.

Spaceman   What about the numbers?

Moonman   No, the voice . . . the . . .

Pause.

Spaceman   Company?

This computes for **Spaceman***: this man is motivated by loneliness. And it's too close to the bone for* **Moonman***.*

Moonman   Tell me about what happened to your comms again. Broke them with a spanner, you say?

Spaceman   I don't want to talk about that.

Moonman   What do you want to talk about?

Spaceman   About when you're getting me down from here.

Moonman   We could talk about space. While we're waiting. About (*whispers*) *the programme*.

Spaceman   I hate to disappoint, Moonman, but I'm not on this programme, whatever it is.

Pause.

And what is this programme?

Moonman   First: back to the Moon! Fifty craft land there to construct a base. Cannibalising those fifty will create ten new craft powered by *a new type of fuel* made from water at the Moon's poles. Mars then within five years and from those ten one new craft – unlike anything seen before – will explore the universe. You're part of the fifty. Maybe you'll be on one of the ten. Maybe even the one. Maybe I can go along with you part of the way. If you brought your radio.

Just the one thing . . . one thing I don't understand. Why did you cut your comms with Earth?

Spaceman *appears to change the subject.*

Spaceman   You know I met this chick . . . a woman, in a bar, before this mission. Asked me what I did. I told her. You know what she said?

Moonman *tee-hees.*

Moonman   'Is that a rocket in your pocket?'

Spaceman   She said: 'Oh, are they still doing that?'

Moonman   Some people!

But your comms –

Spaceman   I blame the white coats. We thought the answers were out there. But all the while the scientists were thinking: no, they're in here, in the atoms. We don't need you guys with the muscles, all we need is a big microscope. And then it was electrons and positrons and pretty soon mesons and quarks and the Higgs goddamn boson.

And we're no closer to answering the Big Questions. I'm not sure I can remember what they were in the first place. To help Mankind reach its potential, something like that. Better, bolder people with bigger brains and bigger balls. If we weren't going to find the answers at least we were going to spend our lives trying. *Give* our lives trying. That is a thing for a man to do. I had a mission, Moonman: to be so fit, so brave, so smart I was barely human – Jesus, some days I thought I could feel something under my skin busting to get out. Like wings. Not just for me. Even for the likes of you.

Moonman *is irked.*

Moonman   The likes of me, eh? Even for the likes of me . . .

Mind you, I don't think I'd take a spanner to my – [spacecraft]

Spaceman   I did it because . . .

Because . . .

Because . . .

Even though . . . even though all that shit we . . .

Even though . . .

It was a present, to myself, ok? A retirement present.

Moonman   Oh, retiring, are you?

Congratulations.

I'm not sure I understand.

Spaceman   Not sure I do.

Because . . . because . . .

You know we have a lander on Mars?

Moonman   The Mars Rover! I knew it! I knew you were involved in – [that]

Spaceman   You know what they're doing up there?

Moonman   It's taking samples.

Spaceman   Samples, yeah. And what's another word for that? Scooping up dust.

Moonman   I don't know . . . digging?

Spaceman   And what's another word for digging, on a massive scale?

Moonman   I don't know. Shovelling! . . . excavating . . .

Spaceman   Mining.

That's why they're all dying to get there, Chinese soon. Not to see if there once was water. Not to see if there once was life. To see if they can dig for minerals to make cell phones . . . so people can watch . . . dancing cats . . . suck dick.

We thought that the answers were out there. We were going to find something *special* – not special, special isn't special enough – something un*earth*ly. But all we did was just smear our own shit over space.

That answer your question?

Wanna know my mission, Moonman? To test the effect of zero gravity on enzymes.

Moonman   Zero gravity!

Spaceman   To test the effect of zero gravity on enzymes in order to develop nanotechnologies.

Moonman   Nanotechnologies!

Spaceman   To test the effect of zero gravity on enzymes in order to develop nanotechnologies . . . in laundry detergent.

He chews his bitter cud for a moment, then reveals his intent.

So if you think you've caught yourself a unicorn in a bear trap, Moonman, if you think you've caught yourself a little fairy in a jar, I'm sorry but I have to disappoint.

Losing you, *buddy.*

Spaceman *switches off.*

Scene Eight

Spaceman *checks his countdown clock – he's content enough with what he sees. He resumes working on his comms. He is making progress. While doing so, he sings the carol 'I Wonder as I Wander' to himself in a cracked voice.*

Spaceman
  I wonder as I wander out under the sky,
  How Jesus the Saviour did come for to die.
  For poor orn'ry people like you and like I . . .
  I wonder as I wander out under the sky.

He unravels the spaghetti of wires.

Ohhhh . . . K.

He works on the wiring. He clips out a damaged section. There is a spurt of activity – fizzes, squawks – which then dies.

Power? Check.

Signal?

He holds out the two wires that need to touch. He pulls on them. They are just short of connecting. **Spaceman** *hunts around for cable – nada. But then it occurs to him where there is some.*

Ha!

Spaceman *lifts the ham radio and is about to use his screwdriver on it when* **Moonman** *bursts through the speaker – it's as if* **Spaceman** *were holding* **Moonman**'s *head in his hands, and he has a screwdriver.*

Moonman   I can't.

Over?

Over?

I just can't.

Over?

Spaceman   Can't what?

Moonman   Go out.

Spaceman   What, you got a flat tyre now too?

Moonman   I just can't go out.

Spaceman   Even to save a man's life. One person on Earth I can get hold of and they're –

Moonman   I don't use a wheelchair.

Pause.

Spaceman   You . . . creep.

Moonman   I can walk.

Spaceman   You pathetic creep.

Moonman   I just can't go out.

Spaceman   What kind of a . . . creep . . . pretends he's in a wheelchair?

Moonman   I just can't.

Spaceman   Wait, no, I get this. You're such a pathetic creep no one wants to know you. And now you think you're going to keep me up here hanging on the line . . .

Moonman   I'm 12-34.

Spaceman   That CB for 'creep', *10-4*? I know all about creeps like you, holding people hostage, getting off on it. Kinda creep keeps little girls in the basement . . .

Moonman   I'm 12-34 . . . not right. In the head.

Spaceman   You're right there, *buddy*.

Moonman   I can't go out. I've got agoraphobia.

Spaceman   That's funny, I've got patheticcreepophobia. It only comes on when I'm talking to you . . .

Moonman   Shut up. Shut up!

Spaceman   Don't tell me to shut up you . . . pussy. You think you're going to keep me here so you've got someone to talk to? I mean, what kind of person –

Moonman   Exactly! What kind of astronaut smashes up their own ship?!

One that doesn't really want to come back down.

Down to Earth.

With a bump.

This lands.

You know, I was thinking. That job in the bank . . . give you a choice between a job in a bank and . . . do you have a background in financial services? I mean they don't give out those jobs to anyone.

But I was thinking. With your interest in fuels. You could get a job with a petrol company.

I'm not talking about in a petrol station, like, on the forecourt. In the office. Not the office out the back of the petrol station, the *head* office, maybe.

Maybe not the *head* office.

Spaceman   I have almost fixed my comms, Moonman. All I need is one inch of cable for the wires to touch.

Moonman   Regional office, but handier to where you live. With the chair . . . and the . . . desk. And the . . . filing cabinet.

Spaceman   But you know where I got cable? Do you know where there's slack? In fact, it's all slack. Redundancy. Just useless matter just taking up space. In this radio.

Moonman   It's worse than being in a wheelchair! It's . . . the door! You know what an event horizon is? Of course you do. The point of no return around a black hole.

Spaceman *hates hearing him talk about the terrors of space again.*

Spaceman   Don't start with that shit again!

Moonman   Nothing is certain about a black hole. Space and time are warped. The only thing certain about a black hole is that once you cross the event horizon you will be sucked into annihilation.

Spaceman   You don't have a black hole outside your door. But *I* do. You aren't running out of fuel and are about to leave earth orbit but *I* – [am]

Moonman   I know there's no black hole . . . If I go to the door I start thinking about how I'm going to feel. Even if I say to myself, particularly if I say to myself, 'I have nothing to fear outside this door' . . . then I'm reminding myself of what I'm going to feel outside the door. How do I stop thinking about how I'm going to feel outside the door? By not thinking about it? How do you not think about a thought without thinking about not thinking about it and so you're thinking about it? You're just spiralling round it, round and round and getting closer and closer and . . . *that*'s an event horizon.

Spaceman   Moonman, there isn't a black hole outside your door.

Moonman   I know! It's in my head! Can you think of a worse place?

This lands for a moment with **Spaceman**. *For a moment . . .*

Spaceman   For God's sake, Moonman! Do you ever think about anybody but yourself? Someone pretty soon is going to be suffocated.

He looks at his countdown clock.

I've got just shy of one orbit left, so someone pretty soon *will* be spiralling, spiralling out of orbit. Just cause you're scared.

Moonman   You're the one who's scared! Scared of floating off into space when that's what you want! Like some pioneer craft, to be the first, the special boy. But to do that you have to be sucked into infinite black than darker than empty than black.

But maybe there are things that are darker than black. More suffocating than space. Things worse than dying.

But, you know, we'll be just the same, when you come down. Even if you get that job . . . me and you, the chair, the desk, lights coming on of an afternoon . . . putting your neck through the millstone every morning . . . and the weighted suit with it . . . the gravity boots where you can hardly put one foot in front of the other. And you'll . . . trudge into the 'void', is it? All whatchamacallit . . . *meaning*, all *thingymebob* . . . purpose, all self . . . is it 'annihilated' is the word?

I know where your black hole is. It's waiting for you, in a drawer in a desk in an office, *special boy.*

They both simultaneously disconnect.

Spaceman *is left looking at his countdown clock in a new light.*

Scene Nine

Spaceman *has taken the panel off the ham radio. Maybe sets screwdrivers down.*

He gets up and walks off a few steps (if desirable in performance, given zero gravity). He mimes a routine that we initially think is to do with his role in the spacecraft: returns a few steps, opens an imaginary door.

Spaceman   Door.

Check.

He advances, sits in his chair.

Chair. Check.

He arranges imaginary pens and paper, even an imaginary photograph of his ex-wife and kids, looks at it, maybe turns it away.

Desk . . .

He is trapped by the inexorable gravity of its black hole.

Moonman *looks up at space, his FM radio burbling in the background.*

Moonman   Could have been me.

Up there.

In a tin can.

Doing 'push-ups'.

Spaceman *valiantly returns to the ham radio. He stares at it, about to work on it, when he is distracted by thoughts of* **Moonman**, *speaks into its gubbins.*

Spaceman   I mean what kind of person would [do that]? How . . . lonely . . . do you have to be?

He glances at his countdown clock. He gives up on the radio for the time being.

He unzips a pocket and takes out an old letter. He reads it like he has read it many times before.

In Donegal, something catches **Moonman**'s *ear on the FM radio.*

Presenter   McGovern, Michaela. Suddenly at home.

Moonman *jumps.*

Moonman   Jesus!

He turns the radio up.

Presenter   Her blessed remains will be interred after 10 o'clock mass, alongside her sister Antoinette.

Pause. Will there be a comical prayer?

Presenter   If I may . . . 'Will those who think of her today, a little prayer to Jesus say.'

Spaceman *carefully folds up the letter and puts it back in his pocket.*

Moonman *frantically tries to get hold of* **Spaceman**.

Moonman   Moonman calling Spaceman, over?

Over?

Are you still there?

You know, I was thinking, over?

There are loads of things you could do. Product endorsements, opening . . . things. You know, not like

opening . . . tins . . . ha! . . . opening whole *supermarkets*! No,
I mean, interviews and things . . .

Pause, then **Spaceman** *responds.*

Spaceman   We have a word for that guy.

Moonman   Oh, thank God!

Spaceman   Living off past glories. We call that guy a Nass-
hole.

Moonman   Oh, ha! A Nasa-hole! Brilliant!

But you could tell your side of the story – interviews – about,
you know . . . they're bound to ask you about, you know, the
comms, but –

Spaceman   Yeah, there goes that job in the bank.

He chews the truth of this; **Moonman** *repents of his previous
taunting.*

Moonman   Nah, fella like you could get a job doing
anything. They'd be queuing up to . . . The thing with the
wires . . . the inch of cable you needed . . . still working on
that?

Pause, then off the bottom of this head:

Spaceman   I've got a thing with a switch.

I'll figure it out.

Moonman   I'm going to get you someone.

Spaceman   Let's just talk.

He puts a clipboard over his screen, obscuring his countdown clock.

Moonman   Right now.

Moonman *stares at a pile of old papers and magazines on his desk.*

Spaceman   That's what you want, isn't it? Talk? I mean,
who knows if we'll get another chance?

Moonman *stops looking at the pile.*

Moonman   What do you want to talk about?

Spaceman   You wanna know who the real hero of space is?

The *Voyager* spacecraft, both of them, still out there years after they were supposed to fail. *Voyager 1* is still sending signals back. Rode the termination shock at the edge of the solar system, burst through the heliosheath, crossed the heliopause and tasted the interstellar medium for the first time. To see that . . . to be the first to see that.

It's in *inter-stellar* space now . . . and it's still sending its beeps back.

Used to be five investigation teams analysing its data. Now there's one.

And you know what it's saying to them? Its numbers are saying that its attitude control is off!

He laughs. He laughs harder.

Moonman   What's funny about that?

Spaceman   It's saying that its comms antenna isn't pointed at Earth!

Moonman   Ha!

I don't get it.

Spaceman   But if its comms antenna wasn't pointed at Earth . . .

It's like the one about the dumb guy says to the deaf guy 'I can't speak' and the deaf guy says 'That's ok, I can't hear you anyway'.

If its antenna wasn't pointed at Earth they couldn't receive the signal saying its antenna isn't pointed at Earth! It's a joke – it's a wind-up, it's a fuck-you. *Voyager 1* has evolved consciousness and its first words are to flip Earth the bird!

Moonman   Are you saying that's why you smashed your thing? To give Earth the fingers?

Spaceman *thinks. He doesn't precisely know what he's saying.*

Spaceman   I'm just talking.

Moonman   I'm going to get you someone. I'm going to get hold of someone right now.

Spaceman   Who's coming now, the other sister?

Moonman   Ah, no. That would be a negatory now.

Spaceman   No?

Moonman   Been bad, with her nerves, past while . . .

That can be bad for the heart.

Spaceman   Heart attack?

Not . . . dead, is she?!

Moonman   Well, they're burying her day after tomorrow.

Spaceman   Christ, Moonman.

Moonman   Don't you worry, I'll get you someone.

Spaceman   That's not necessarily what I was worried about.

Moonman   Oh don't you worry about me. You worry about you.

I have a press in the kitchen the full of tins.

Pause. **Spaceman** *finds he wants to talk; he has no one else to talk it out with.*

Moonman   I'm going to get you someone right – [now]

Spaceman   Katrina.

My wife. Was on the NASA programme with me.

Moonman   You have a wife?!

Spaceman   Ex.

PhD from MIT, BMI of 19, I had 100 dollars on her as the
first female astronaut. Guy in medical kept calling her the
'oestronaut' behind her back. She just laughed and called his
wife and said he'd won a Subaru. We watched from a café
across the street as he rocked up for the presentation.

Moonman   I thought Sally Ride was the first lady astronaut.

Spaceman   Took time out to have the kids.

Moonman   You have children?!

Spaceman   Grown-up, live their own lives. Let's say I was
out of town a lot.

She was rostered for the *Challenger* STS-32. PR liked the fact
she was a mother and all. But she walked out. Couple years
later, walked out on me. Wrote me a 'Dear John'.

The actual words of the great Katrina Hiesterman were:
'The challenge is to live *life*, not something that isn't life.
What better enterprise could men invent for avoiding life
than space travel?! The challenge is to live in *this* world, not a
new one.'

What a . . . what a . . .

Moonman   'Bitch'?

Spaceman   That's what I thought.

What a *challenge*!

Hard though.

Hardest.

It's too hard for him. He accepts this.

'We can explore other worlds just as soon as we've exhausted
the possibilities of doing something about this one.'

They sit in the moment.

Moonman   It's worse than being in a wheelchair, you know.

Spaceman   Forget about it.

Moonman   If you're in a wheelchair at least –

Spaceman   How long you been like this? When was the last time you left the house?

Moonman *gnaws his paws, folds.*

Moonman   A while.

Spaceman   A week, a month, a year?

Moonman   Eight.

Spaceman   Years?

He takes this in.

You been in therapy?

Moonman   I was supposed to go and see the big doctor but . . . you know . . . and these fellas are too busy to make house calls . . .

Spaceman   Jeez, Moonman . . .

He thinks, then puts the headset on.

OK, let's get some tools out, see if we can't make some running repairs.

Moonman   You're not a doctor.

Spaceman   Fuck doctors.

Let's get to the bottom of this. Now you know there's nothing out there.

Moonman   That's the problem.

Spaceman   No, there's not nothing out there. There's plenty. I've been where there's supposed to be nothing – there's plenty.

Moonman   There's cars and people and dogs, but beyond that . . .

Spaceman   No, we just been through that.

Moonman   When you were a kid, did you ever think about space?

Spaceman   I'm asking the questions.

Moonman   You're a kid so you're sitting on the stairs trying to work out what it's all about. Third stair up, Ardree Cottage, Townland Drumany Lower, Letterkenny, County Donegal, Ireland, Europe, the World, the Universe . . . what's bigger than the Universe? . . . nothing . . . the Universe goes on and on . . . where does it stop? It doesn't. It's infinite and you feel so . . .

Spaceman   Excited?

Moonman   And then maybe you spot your face in the hall mirror and you come rushing back . . . whoosh . . . from the Universe to third stair up, into you, whatever that is . . . and your face is burning and you need to sit down to the toilet . . . how can anything be infinite? What are you? Some speck of dirt?

Spaceman   We don't know the universe is infinite. There could be something beyond it.

Moonman   And beyond that?

Spaceman   Something else.

Moonman   And beyond that? Stretching into infinity?

Spaceman   Or there could be nothing.

Moonman   Or nothing. What kind of choice is that: between infinity and nothing? How can you feel that your feet are touching the ground, that you're even here, if the choice is between infinity, I can't think what infinity is, and nothing, I can't think what nothing is either. You tell me there's something out there? There's nothing. Or infinity.

Spaceman   What you got is depersonalisation. We learn about this psych stuff.

There's plenty out there. Plenty of real stuff that you can touch, and feel . . .

Now tell me what happens when you open the door. And no space nonsense.

Moonman It's a black hole.

Spaceman What did I just say?

What you got is free-floating anxiety. Now that's got nothing to do with floating away into infinity or nothing. What it means is something is scaring you – not the door, not the outside – but you can't remember what it is. So you get scared of the outside instead. Tell me about your mother.

Moonman What's my mother got to do with it? What about *your* mother?

Spaceman She thought I was special. She's dead. Tell me about your mother.

Moonman She thought I was special. I loved her.

Spaceman And did she love you?

Moonman Of course she loved me, I was her son.

Spaceman Did she tell you?

Moonman Yes, actually she did.

Spaceman Your dad? He tell you?

Moonman Yes, every night he would say 'I love you, son'. And every morning: 'Good morning, son, I love you'. And in the pub: 'Wanna-pint-son-I-love-you-do-you-want-a-half 'un-with-that-I-love-you-I fancy-this-Irish-horse-at-Cheltenham-did-I-tell-you-that-I-loved you?'.

Spaceman I take it that's a 'no'. You think about that a lot, that your father didn't love you?

Moonman No . . .

Spaceman   Aha! You see, it's going to be something you *don't* think about . . . He ever, you know . . .

Moonman   I'm switching off here. I'm switching off, you filthy . . . American.

Spaceman   Raw nerve?

Talk to me. Come on.

Moonman   You want to know about my mammy and daddy? You won't like what you hear . . .

Spaceman   Oh I heard it all.

Moonman   1968, my father came home with an old Morris Minor. He had an oul' pony and trap that had been his father's and the pony was famous for knowing the way home from the pub if he fell asleep . . .

Spaceman   Drinker, was he?

Moonman   He liked a pint.

Spaceman   And when he came home? Mean?

Moonman   He sang! Sometimes we'd sing along with him! So he comes home one day having spent a few bob on this oul' car.

Spaceman   Was your mom angry?

Moonman   What use had he for a car only to take us on day trips? So the idea was to set off in the morning for Donegal town. Except that we didn't get away until midday because it took that long for my mother to get ready. So he's out there in the Morris, checking the tyre pressure, re-checking the oil. And when she comes out she gives him the look: 'Don't you dare accuse me of making you late.' So she gets in and not a word except he tells her there's a map in the glove compartment.

Spaceman   What happened that day?

Moonman   Three hours later we're in Magheroarty – miles
out of the way. And my daddy's trying not to say anything,
and my mammy's boiling away because he doesn't *need* to say
it, she can hear it going through his head: 'You got us lost.'
And she's dying to say: 'Well, it's you that's driving.' And then
he says it: 'I'd been better with the pony.' Now what he
meant was: 'I'd have been better taking us there in the pony
and trap.' But what she heard was: 'I should have brought
the pony instead of you – *it* would have known the way.' 'Stop
the car,' she says. 'If you value your pony more than me then
it can do all your washing and cooking.'

Spaceman   Your mom and dad didn't get along.

Moonman   But she doesn't get out and after a minute he
switches on the engine again, except now it won't start.
Anyway, we got to Donegal Town 10 o'clock that night. My
daddy gave me the money for the dodgems. We all got one.
My mother, driving into the back of him with this 'I'm-not-
laughing-not-yet' face.

Spaceman   And the point is?

Moonman   She brought us to the Abbey Hotel so Daddy
could have a pint for the drive home and there was a picture
of President Kennedy on the wall and they got talking about
the time he visited, me with my crisps and my nose in my
new comic, and then they were whispering about what it was
like the time of the nuclear missile crisis and what nearly
happened.

Spaceman   The Cuban Missile Crisis?! Is that the point?

Moonman   It was dark driving home and they thought I
was sleeping and my mother was singing.

(*Sings.*)
　　For love is pleasing and love is teasing,
　　And love is a treasure when first 'tis new

and she was stroking my father's cheek.

There we were snug in this little bubble, a little bubble of a car, a little bubble of love under the stars. But this sadness in her voice, always this sadness in the twilight. And I suddenly knew what it was. This has to end. And I wished, I truly wished, there could be some nuclear bomb to take us all away. Together.

Spaceman   That's it? That's the point of your shaggy dog story?

Moonman   That's what I think about when I think about them. They put my daddy in a wheelchair. I was relieved when he went, God forgive me.

Spaceman   What about women?

Moonman   You think I should have left my mother on her own after that? Is that what they call love in your country?

Spaceman   There would have been places for your mother . . .

Moonman   I would have chewed my own hands off before I would have put my mother in a home.

Spaceman   Interesting. You'd have chewed your paws off like a bear in a trap . . .

Moonman   Of course I felt trapped! I *was* trapped. And he was trapped and she was trapped and you're trapped and we're all trapped!

Near ten years to the day she went too and her eyes saying I love you and I don't want to leave you on your own but even love can't overcome this . . .

Spaceman *waits for more.*

Spaceman   Is this what you want to tell me? That's what's wrong with you? That you loved your mom and dad and they died?

Moonman   You brought them up.

Spaceman   If it is, I have to tell you, Moonman, that that is life. We're all going to die. You're going to die, I'm going to die.

Moonman   Yes, but you got to live first!

Spaceman *thinks.*

Spaceman   That's true. I got to be an astronaut.

But maybe the challenge is to live *this* life . . .

. . . huddle up tight. Together.

Sounds like you had the good stuff. And you lost it. I had it and I gave it away . . . got this in return.

He takes a moment to swallow this.

Maybe you can get it again somehow.

Moonman   *I can't leave.*

Spaceman   Way I see it, staying there ain't working out for you.

Moonman   I can't!

Spaceman   Ain't no can't in *Can*averal.

Moonman   No!

Spaceman   Ain't no 'no' in Apoll*o*!

Moonman*'s phone rings. Nice and loud and old-fashioned from under the pile of papers.* **Moonman** *scrambles to answer it.* **Spaceman** *is dumbstruck.*

Moonman   Hello?

Yes.

No.

No, I got the double-glazing in a while ago. Thanks, bye, bye-bye, bye.

He hangs up.

(*To* **Spaceman**.) I swear to God, I was just going to phone for you. I swear on my mother and father's lives. I'm going to ring them, right now, while you're on the line . . . are you still on the line? Over?

Spaceman *slowly takes his headset off, switches to speaker/remote mic.*

Spaceman   I've moved on to Plan B.

Moonman   Plan B?

Spaceman   Suppose I've had it in my back pocket . . . till now.

Problem was that since comms went down with Earth the computer didn't have a signal to follow to get me home. But it does. A radio signal. Yours. All programmed in. All I got to do is bale out, splash down in the capsule in (*reads from screen*) . . . 'Lough Swilly' . . . before the ship itself lands.

Moonman   Lands? Where?

Spaceman   Well, 'crashes' would be a better word. Into you in your field. Hope you got home insurance.

Moonman   You . . . you . . .

Spaceman   Fuck you.

Moonman   You can't do that.

Spaceman   Call the police. Call the fucking postman.

Moonman   You can't do that.

Spaceman   Resourceful guys, astronauts.

Moonman   You wouldn't!

Spaceman   I'm a desperate man.

Moonman   I . . . *can't* . . . leave!

Spaceman   I . . . *don't* . . . care.

I already started the landing initiation sequence.

Moonman   I told you!

Spaceman   Yes, you told me. There was a black hole outside your door. I've got news for you: there is. It's weird and it's terrifying and it doesn't follow any of the laws of physics, not inside your head where it matters, and you get sucked into it and you never get out alive. It's called life.

Moonman   I –

You'll never make it.

Spaceman   You don't get it, do you? I don't care. What I want is to crash twenty-four tons of metal into the top of your head! Burn you alive with a fuel that burns hotter than the sun!

Moonman, *panicked, moves from his desk in the direction of the door.*

Moonman   You can't . . . you *wouldn't* . . .

I don't believe you.

Spaceman   Be coming up on Lough Swilly any minute! You might even be able to see me!

Moonman *gets to the door, turns his back to it.*

Moonman   No!

Spaceman   Remember: it's not normal out there, no matter what anybody told you. It's *weird*. It's *terrifying*. More empty than colder than blacker than infinite nothing. You're *right*.

He turns to face the door.

Moonman   Like an EVA. Like a spacewalk.

Spaceman   Like a spacewalk.

Spaceman's *craft appears to roar.*

I can see the lights of a town.

So . . . you going to open the hatch?

Moonman   I – [can't]

He twigs **Spaceman** *is trying to help him.*

I'm not stupid, you know. I might not have a PhD from MIT but I'm not a stupid person. You can't do that. Follow some random radio signal to Earth.

Spaceman *gives up.*

Moonman   Why did you do that to me?

Spaceman   Oh, you know.

That was brave, man. You almost did it.

Moonman   Don't patronise me.

Spaceman   I'm sorry.

But it is . . . you're prepared to die there rather than go out . . . brave. Made a call; stuck with it. They're going to find you there someday, all shrunk up, desiccated, alone . . .

Moonman   At least they'll find me.

You're not going home, are you?

Spaceman *declines to answer.* **Moonman** *hears roaring from* **Spaceman**'s *craft.*

Moonman   What's that sound?

Spaceman   That?

We hear in the background:

Computer   Oxygen! Oxygen! Oxygen!

Spaceman   That is the sound of a hatch depressurising.

He removes the clipboard obscuring the orbital countdown and shuts the laptop.

We need to be brave, don't we?

Moonman   I thought the challenge was to 'live life'.

Spaceman   Can't do it. They made me out of wires and tin
. . . and worn-out stories of knights of old.

I'm going out there.

Moonman   Like *Voyager*.

That's what you want?

Spaceman   I think that's what I always wanted.

I'll send you beeps, yeah? Listen out for my beeps. Static and
beeps, that's all there is . . . all we need . . . I dunno.

Will you listen out?

Moonman *is silent*.

Spaceman   Talk to me. I'm scared.

Will you listen out?

Moonman   I will, yeah.

What's your name?

Spaceman   Commander –

My name is Slane.

Paul Slane.

Paul.

Moonman   Denis.

Spaceman *puts on his helmet, moves toward his hatch*.

Spaceman   Hello, Denis.

Moonman   Hello, Paul.

He gets up, moves toward his door.

Spaceman   Bye-bye, Denis.

Moonman   Bye-bye, Paul.

A greater roar.

Spaceman   Your mom ever sing 'I Wonder as I Wander' to you? It's Scotch-Irish.

Moonman   Don't know it.

Spaceman *sings through the roar of space and static.*

Spaceman (*sings*)
    I wonder as I wander out under the sky,
    How Jesus the Saviour did come for to die.
    For poor orn'ry people like you and like I . . .

Come on!

Sing to me.

(*Sings.*)
    I wonder as I . . .

Spaceman/Moonman (*sing*)
    wander out under the sky,
    How Jesus the Saviour did come for to die.
    For poor orn'ry people like you and like I . . .
    I wonder as I wander out under the sky

Both face the open doors and the mute roar of space. **Spaceman** *puts his visor down.*

Moonman (*sings*)
    I wander as I wonder . . .
    I wonder as I wander . . .

Paul? Paul?

He's gone.

Moonman *stands on the brink. The door opens into the dark. The hint of a movement forward that could always be reversed.*

Blackout. Static.

www.ingramcontent.com/pod-product-compliance
Lightning Source LLC
Chambersburg PA
CBHW041922090426
42741CB00019B/3450